Joseph Carson

A Discourse Commemorative of the Life and Character of

Samuel Jackson

Joseph Carson

A Discourse Commemorative of the Life and Character of Samuel Jackson

ISBN/EAN: 9783337816445

Printed in Europe, USA, Canada, Australia, Japan

Cover: Foto ©Thomas Meinert / pixelio.de

More available books at **www.hansebooks.com**

A DISCOURSE

COMMEMORATIVE OF THE LIFE AND CHARACTER

OF

SAMUEL JACKSON, M.D.,

LATE PROFESSOR OF THE INSTITUTES OF MEDICINE

IN THE

UNIVERSITY OF PENNSYLVANIA.

BY

JOSEPH CARSON, M.D.,
PROFESSOR OF MATERIA MEDICA AND PHARMACY.

DELIVERED OCTOBER 7, 1872,

BEFORE THE

TRUSTEES, PROFESSORS, AND STUDENTS OF THE UNIVERSITY OF PENNSYLVANIA.

PHILADELPHIA:
COLLINS, PRINTER, 705 JAYNE STREET.
1872.

CORRESPONDENCE.

At a meeting of the Medical Class of the University of Pennsylvania, held Oct. 12th, 1872, for the purpose of requesting a copy of Prof. Joseph Carson's Introductory Lecture, Mr. Charles K. I. Miller, of Pennsylvania, was called to the Chair, and Mr. Wm. H. Rush, of Philadelphia, appointed Secretary.

On motion it was

Resolved, That committees be appointed to carry out the intention of the Class.

> UNIVERSITY OF PENNSYLVANIA,
> Philadelphia, Oct. 14, 1872.

JOSEPH CARSON, M.D., *Prof. of Materia Medica, University of Penna.*

DEAR SIR : At a meeting of the Medical Class, held on the 12th inst., the following gentlemen were appointed a committee to solicit for publication a copy of your address, delivered as an introductory to the one hundred and seventh course of lectures, in eulogy of the late Prof. Samuel Jackson, of this school.

> ENRIQUE M. ESTRAZULAS, Uruguay, South America.
> JOHN G. SCHENCK, New Jersey.
> JUAN GUITERAS, Cuba.
> EDWARD T. BRUEN, Pennsylvania.
> FRANK C. HAND, Pennsylvania.

> UNIVERSITY OF PENNSYLVANIA,
> Philadelphia, Oct. 15th, 1872.

To Messrs. ESTRAZULAS, SCHENCK, GUITERAS, BRUEN, and HAND, Committee of Medical Class.

GENTLEMEN : I accede with pleasure to the request of the Medical Class, expressed through you, that the Eulogy of the late Professor Jackson, delivered at the opening of the Session, should be published under its auspices.

Be pleased to convey to the Class my appreciation of the feeling expressed by the request, and the assurance of my deep interest in your welfare and that of your fellow students.

> Very sincerely your
> obedient servant,
> J. CARSON.

COMMITTEE ON PUBLICATION.

GUILHERME ELLIS, S. Paulo, Brazil, S. A.
CYRUS A. LOOSE, Pennsylvania.
JAMES S. EVERTON, Pennsylvania.
CHAS. P. BRITTON, New Jersey.
FRANK HOUSKEEPER, Pennsylvania.
H. TURNER BASS, N. C.
JOHN S. BAGG, Massachusetts.
WM. A. BELL, Virginia.
EMILE S. BUNWILL, Delaware.
WESTWOOD J. BAKER, Alabama.
HERBERT R. CARTER, N. B.
JOHN M. STEELE, Md.
CHAS. C. MATTESON, Ill.
HENRY ESSIG, Mo.
WILLIAM GAMBLE, Conn.
WM. P. D. GILTNER, Oregon.
BRADY O. WILLIAMS, W. Virg.

REUBEN W. GULLEDGE, Miss.
LYCURTAS B. HALL, Vermont.
EDWARD J. HALLUM, Texas.
JOSEPH C. HUNTER, Iowa.
FRANCIS J. ROGERS, R. I.
WM. T. WYTHE, Cal.
HERMAN N. LOEB, Chili, S. A.
GEORGE H. LAMSON, France.
WALTER H. LEWIS, Ind.
RICHARD T. METCALFE, Nova Scotia.
KENKICHE R. MAYEDA, Japan.
ABR. A. McDONALD, Minn.
ROBERT PILLOW, Tenn.
V. GONZALES SALINAS, Mexico.
THADDEUS F. TRUMAN, N. Y.
JAMES F. WATSON, Ky.
EDWARD JECKELL, England.

WM. H. RUSH,
Secretary.

CHAS. K. I. MILLER,
Chairman.

A DISCOURSE.

A FAITHFUL record of the lives of men who have borne a prominent part in the affairs of the world, who have been remarkable not only for their eminence in professional pursuits, but for the length of time that they have been engaged in them, is of twofold interest.

Such a record not only exhibits to us the steps by which individual success and reputation have been attained; but it is interwoven with the history of the times through which they passed. It entails a narrative of events of general concern, of changes which have exercised an important influence upon the progress of mankind, and of improvements and discoveries which have contributed to the expansion and perfection of positive knowledge. From these alone, when estimated in their fulness, the evidence can be drawn of the advances made by generation upon generation in the march of science and of civilization.

It will be the purpose of the present effort to thus sketch the life of the eminent physician and teacher, who, for so long a period, was conspicuous before his fellow-men as a promoter of professional advancement, and who was especially distinguished as an ornament and sustainer of this school of medicine.

Dr. Samuel Jackson was born in the city of Philadelphia, on March 22d, 1787. He was the son of Dr. David Jackson of Chester County, Penna., who was one of the first class of graduates on whom the degree of Bachelor of Medicine was conferred by the College of Philadelphia in 1768, and subsequently a Trustee of the Institution. His mother was Susan Kemper, the daughter of Jacob Kemper, who came to this country from Germany in 1741, and settled in New Jersey.

This lady lived to the age of eighty-eight years; indeed longevity seems to have been incident to the descent, as her father lived to the age of eighty-seven years, and her son to that of eighty-five.[1] She was remarkable for her powers of conversation, a trait that, in an eminent degree, was inherited by her son.

Dr. Jackson acquired his classical education in the University of Pennsylvania, the institution that had succeeded the College, but he does not appear to have taken any literary degrees. He began the study of medicine with Dr. James Hutchinson, Jr., but this gentleman, who was remarkable for his mechanical ingenuity, dying shortly after the connection commenced, he was transferred to the office of Professor Wistar, with whom he completed his studies. He received the degree of Doctor of Medicine from the University, in 1808. His Thesis was "Suspended Animation."

After his graduation Dr. Jackson did not enter upon the practice of his profession. His father had been engaged in the business of a druggist and pharmaceutist, and, having died in 1801, its continuance devolved on his eldest son. Upon the death of this brother in 1809, Dr. Jackson continued the business, rendered necessary from the dependent state of the family. The details of trade, however, were never congenial to the tastes of our late professor; he was clearly unadapted to such pursuits, and his aspirations took a higher flight. He was not in the least endowed with the mercantile spirit, and was little fitted to push his fortunes in a remunerative field, whence others have drawn wealth and independence. As soon as he could do so he abandoned the occupation of a pharmaceutist, and became a candidate for practice and reputation in his legitimate profession. To his credit it may be stated, that when he retired from business, being deeply involved pecuniarily, he regarded all his obligations with a

[1] The longevity of this family is remarkable. Jacob Kemper died at the age of 87 years; Mrs. Morton, his daughter, at 93 years; Col. Daniel Kemper, his son, at 98 years; Mrs. Jackson, his daughter, at 89; Bishop Kemper, his grandson, at 81 years; Mrs. Quincey, his granddaughter, at 77 years, and Samuel Jackson, his grandson, at 85 years.

sense of honor, and subsequently liquidated them from his professional earnings, with principal and interest.

While engaged in business pursuits, the war of 1812 with Great Britain was declared. Dr. Jackson had always been an adherent of the Jefferson school of politics, the principles of which he imbibed from his father, and, as a member of the Democratic party, which had urged on the contest, was its zealous advocate. He manifested his patriotism by joining the "First Troop of City Cavalry," and with it took part in the advanced movements of the troops then raised to protect the city of Philadelphia from invasion by the British. The autumn and early portion of the winter of 1814 were occupied at Mount Bull, in Maryland, in watching the movements of the enemy, then in the waters of the Chesapeake, or in riding as a vidette between that post and the city. It was after the war had terminated, and peace declared in 1815, that Dr. Jackson closed his business concerns, and by so doing placed himself on a footing with his compeers and brother practitioners in his native city.

Like those of others the fortunes of medical men are various, determined by the circumstances in which they may be placed, by their tastes, and very largely by their idiosyncrasies of character and disposition. It belonged not to Dr. Jackson's mental constitution to remain a passive though meritorious aspirant for public favor; his temperament was ardent, his mind active and inquiring, and he sought the means of advancement by his interest in the well-being of his fellow-citizens, by the application of his knowledge, and by the expenditure of his time in promoting their welfare. Having become a member of the Board of Health of Philadelphia, and chosen its president, a field of distinction and usefulness was presented to him, to be cultivated to the utmost extent of his talents and industry.[1] Events soon proved that the duties of a public servant had not devolved on one incompetent or unequal to their requirements. The opportunity was soon at hand of exhibiting his fitness for his office.

[1] He was elected President of the Board of Health March 20th, 1820. Minutes of Board of Health.

To those who have not gone through the ordeal, there can be no full and real appreciation of the alarm and distress created in a densely populated city by the sudden appearance of such an epidemic as yellow fever. A battle-field has its horrors; they are mitigated, however, by the excitement of the struggle, and the stern discipline of military training: but the unchecked raging of pestilence has unmitigated terrors; it invades the precincts of the family and social circle; it " walketh in darkness," and like a destroying angel it hurries to an untimely end the dearest objects of love or affectionate association. The suddenness of bereavement is appalling and prostrating, and men of the coolest heads and of tried courage are panic-stricken and helpless. To be calm, collected, fearless, and efficient in affording aid and assistance to fellow mortals under such circumstances is godlike.

The epidemics of yellow fever in Philadelphia have called forth the noblest virtues of her medical men, and tested their bravery, their heroic endurance, and their devoted self-sacrifice in behalf of humanity. It is not necessary to detail the trying scenes through which our profession has gone, in connection with the invasion of this scourge, to which so often our city has been subjected. The history of its ravages has been drawn by professional as well as non-professional pens, and fiction even has not exaggerated the delineation. When Dr. Jackson was President of the Board of Health in the summer of 1820, yellow fever, by its sudden and fatal invasion, impressed that body with the weightiness of responsibility that rested upon it; and manfully was this met by its presiding officer and his fellow members.[1] Dr. Jackson identified himself with the efforts of amelioration that were instituted, was a leading counsellor of his fellow practitioners, toiling day and night in thoroughly informing himself as to the nature and character-

---

[1] The members of the Board of Health were,

Samuel Jackson,	Samuel Volens, from City.
Joseph Worrall,	James West,
Franklin Bache,	John Byerly, from Northern Liberties.
William Hawkes,	Charles Souder, Spring Garden.
Jesse R. Burden,	Joshua Raybold, Moyamensing.
	Joel B. Sutherland, Southwark.

isties of the disease, its localities, and its origin and causes; devising, in consultation with his associates, professional and non-professional, the best means of limiting its spread; and has left a graphic and important record, which has placed his name high among the most distinguished and honored contributors to our knowledge of this fearful infliction on the human family. In this work of philanthropy he was ably seconded by Dr. Jesse R. Burden, who was associated with him on the committee of inquiry, and to carry out such sanitary recommendations as were deemed expedient. From exposure to the exciting causes during their exploration, Dr. Jackson had an attack of the disease.[1] Should reference be desired to the papers that were published by Dr. Jackson on the subject, they will be found in the 1st and 2d volumes of the Philadelphia Journal of the Medical and Physical Sciences; and I would further refer to the admirable and exhaustive treatise on yellow fever by Dr. La Roche, in which ample justice is awarded to Dr. Jackson's labors and researches.

Before dismissing this era of Dr. Jackson's life, it may be interesting to make a brief summary of his conclusions. The questions as regards the imported or non-imported origin of yellow fever, and its contagious or non-contagious nature, had long been the subjects of litigation and dispute among medical men, from which had sprung frequently, in the excited state of feeling that was engendered, and from the important interests at stake, not a small amount of acrimony. They were

[1] The following record is on the minutes of the Board of Health, July 26th, 1820: "Resolved that a committee of three be appointed to inspect the present state of the city, included between Arch and Vine Streets, and between Front Street and the Delaware, and report upon the probable causes of the cases of fever which have been reported as existing in that neighborhood, to the Board; and also to take measures to have a daily report of the state of health of all persons employed in the sail loft of Messrs. Keen & Davis, with full powers to remove all nuisances which may come under notice." Messrs. Jackson, Burden and Bache were appointed the committee.

July 29th, 1820, Drs. Jackson and Burden were appointed a committee "to remove persons now living on Hodge's Wharf." August 3d, 1823, fences were directed to be erected.

Dr. Burden had charge of the temporary hospital which was opened July 21st. He resigned September 1st.

questions involving not only the safety and happiness of the community, but affecting its material prosperity. The inroads of death, as well as the increase or decrease of riches, are inseparably connected with them. Can yellow fever be checked at its commencement? Can it be stamped out or prevented? These are points affecting the general welfare. Or, is intercourse with those who are affected with it dangerous, under all circumstances, to the relatives and attendants?—a question that penetrates to the very core of social connection.

It is an interesting fact in the history of the medical profession of Philadelphia, that an association sprang up in 1799 which was called the "Academy of Medicine," and that it had as its founders men who advocated the non-imported and noncontagious origin of yellow fever. Among these were Physick, Dewees, Coxe, Caldwell, and, subsequently, Rush, who had become a convert. This institution was in antagonism to the College of Physicians, in which body the contrary doctrines had their warmest supporters. Before the Academy of Medicine Dr. Jackson read his papers, in 1820. By indefatigable perseverance, and by tracing reports and common rumor to their very source, he had determined that the epidemic of 1820 had not been imported, but that its origin was domestic and local. At the localities where it prevailed he found abundant sources of production in accumulated filth and putrescent animal and vegetable material, and could discover that in no case where individuals laboring under the disease were removed did they propagate it by infection, nor by the sick was it communicated to attendants or relatives who had not been exposed to the same local influences.

The measures which were adopted under his guidance were the removal of all the inhabitants of the infected districts to more salubrious positions, the barricading by fences the localities in which the disease originated, and, as far as practicable, removing offensive matters. In consequence of the measures of the Board of Health, the City Councils were induced, with the aid of the leading medical bodies, to devise such sanitary measures as would prevent a recurrence in future of this calamity. But once since, in 1853, has yellow fever appeared in Philadelphia, and then it was suppressed by prompt and effectual measures.

It may be stated that, while the source and cause of the "black vomit" of yellow fever were subjects of conjecture rather than of scientific research, at the time Dr. Jackson's paper was written, he attributed it to hemorrhage, not to secretion—a view that in later times has been subjected to the full test of chemical and microscopic examination, and has acquired the force of demonstration.

In 1821 the Philadelphia College of Pharmacy entered upon its successful career of operation, and instituted courses of lectures upon chemistry and materia medica, in connection with its plan of educating apprentices in the pharmaceutic art. Dr. Jackson was appointed Professor of Materia Medica, with Dr. Gerard Troost as his colleague in the Chair of Chemistry. The latter gentleman resigned his position the year following, to be succeeded by Professor George B. Wood. This association is worthy of note, when it is recollected that Professors Wood and Jackson, in subsequent years, during a full quarter of a century, were colleagues in this University. The selection of Dr. Jackson to fill the Chair of Materia Medica in the College evidently depended on the estimate of his fitness from his former connection with the pharmaceutic profession, the deep interest he took in the success of the institution, and his share in organizing it. He was the link, as it were, between the two professions, and from early training was supposed to be perfectly conversant with the requirements of each of them. That this was the case, is evident from the whole tenor of the Introductory that he delivered upon entering on his duties.[1]

At the period when the College of Pharmacy was organized the pharmaceutical profession was at a low ebb not only in the city of Philadelphia, but in the United States. When speaking of its condition, in the lecture referred to, he makes this bold and candid declaration: "As respects drugs and medicines, this country, for the last thirty years, has been retrograding rather

---

[1] Dr. Jackson was Chairman of the Committee which presented the plan for the foundation of the College, March 13, 1821. He was elected a Trustee, March 27, 1821, and was on the Committee to draft resolutions for the government of the College.

than advancing. Abandoned by physicians, pharmacology has not been prosecuted as a science by the druggists and apothecaries; no means of instruction were provided for these last, no rules or regulations established for their government in order to insure a correct dispensation of medicines of the most improved and genuine qualities. Individuals engaged in the vocation of an apothecary and druggist without a previous acquaintance with medicines, ignorant of their properties, unconscious of their responsibility and of the fatal effects which might result from their conduct. Anxious to transact business, they have sought to attract customers by the lowness of their prices. Their success compelled others to come down to the same standard, and thus, by successive competition, our drugs and medicines are cheaper than those of Europe, but are deteriorated in the same proportion." But this condition of things was not solely due to the pharmaceutist. "The great body of practitioners, especially those residing in the country, knowing medicines only by their names, have been ignorant of the very different qualities subsisting amongst them. In their purchases, incapable of making a selection as to quality, the lowest price was preferred. Inferior, deteriorated, and sophisticated medicines and drugs met with ready sale, while the choicest and most select, because of higher price, could very seldom meet with a purchaser."

The disheartening picture here presented has been erased, and that such would be the case was predicted by the lecturer. His words were prophetic: "In the United States pharmacology is a new science. Long repudiated from medical instruction, too feeble to assert its claims, neglected and almost forgotten by its more brilliant sister sciences, it has pined in obscurity and penury. This reproach and stain upon the medicine of our country will soon be effaced." For proof that this anticipation has been realized we may proudly survey the present condition of this department throughout the length and breadth of our extended country. The influence of the Philadelphia College of Pharmacy, through its instruction and through its Journal, has been felt in every quarter. It was the pioneer; and other colleges of similar organization have sprung up, in imitation, at the great centres of wealth and population.

The people have been instructed as regards their utility and importance. Co-operation has been effected, and an association among pharmaceutists has been created—the "National Pharmaceutical Association"—which is eminently useful. A Pharmacopœia, whose origin was coeval with the College of Pharmacy, and in which the pharmaceutists are as much interested as are medical men, has become the national standard. Our pharmaceutists may now be ranked among the best instructed of the world.

To whom may be attributed the early planting and nourishment of this intellectual germ which has yielded so plentifully, and has been of such incalculable benefit to the community? The record shows that this was due to the talents, learning, energy, and industry of two members of the medical profession, both subsequently Professors in the University of Pennsylvania, Samuel Jackson and George B. Wood; and further, for the first twenty-five years in the history of the college the duty of instructing its pupils was intrusted to members of the same profession. I wish not to derogate from the merit of those enlightened druggists and apothecaries who were coadjutors in the work of founding the College of Pharmacy. They well appreciated the abilities of those who only at the time could subserve their purpose of instruction, and nobly supported them until eminent members of their own profession arose to carry on the enterprise so happily inaugurated.[1]

---

[1] That the College of Pharmacy did not burst forth a success from its foundation, is shown from the address of Dr. Wood, to the members of the College of Pharmacy, delivered November 16, 1824. The school had then been three years in operation. After stating the requirements for educating an apprentice in the pharmaceutical profession, and the measures that had been adopted, he proceeds to remark: "Professorships on the two most important pharmaceutical sciences have also been instituted, and regular courses of lectures on chemistry and materia medica have been delivered for the last three winters. It would give me great pleasure to be able to tell you that this department of the college is in an equally flourishing condition, but most of you are aware that such an assertion would be an empty boast. The fact is, that, during the last winter more especially, the labors of the lecturers were rewarded by little more than the consciousness that their own share of the necessary duties had not been entirely neglected. The slender expenses incident to the chemical course absorbed, within a very trifling sum, the whole receipts from the students

With respect to a knowledge of pharmacology being necessary to the physician, the language of Dr. Jackson is as applicable and cogent at the present day as it was fully fifty years ago. "No one who reflects upon the subject can question the importance of pharmacological knowledge in the completion of a medical education. Of what avail are talents of the highest order, and erudition the most profound, to a practitioner who is furnished with unfaithful remedies and knows not how to distinguish them? A knowledge of pharmacology is, then, as indispensable to the practitioner as that of any other department of medical science."[1] Dr. Jackson had now fairly entered upon his career as a teacher. Besides holding the chair in the College of Pharmacy, he joined the association which was organized by Dr. Chapman, for the instruction of the pupils of the University who remained in the city during the recess between the public courses of lectures. His first position in it was as teacher of Medical Chemistry, which, on the remodelling of the institution, was changed to that of Materia Medica and Therapeutics. The association alluded to subsequently became the Medical Institute, in which were engaged not only Professors of the University, but some of the most active and rising members of the profession.[2] In 1829 a special hall was erected to accommodate the class, then having reached beyond one hundred in number, and in 1837 a more public and independent character was given to the institution by the bestowal of a charter.

of pharmacy, and the lecturer was denied the pleasure that he himself would have derived from the exhibition of more numerous experiments by the apprehension of actual private loss. He might, indeed, be disposed to attribute this want of encouragement to his own imperfections as a lecturer, but surely the same reason could not be assigned for an almost equal desertion of his colleague. The lectures of the Professor of Materia Medica have never been accused of deficiency, either as to the value of the knowledge inculcated, or as to the manner in which that knowledge is conveyed; he must therefore look to another source for at least a portion of this neglect, and may we not find it in the apathy of a great majority of the members of the college?" Addresses, etc., by George B. Wood, M.D. LL.D.
    Discourse.
   [2] It may be mentioned that the gentlemen thus first united were, Drs. Chapman, Dewees, Horner, Bell, Mitchell, Jackson, Hodge, and Harris.

Dr. Jackson continued his connection with it until in 1844 it was transferred to other hands.

The teaching of Dr. Jackson possessed great attractiveness, not only from its warmth and enthusiasm, but from the freshness and novelty of his prelections and his practical expositions. He exhibited in animated language the ideal entertained by him of the true nature of pharmacological investigation, and placed its proper objects before the mind of the attentive student. Convinced that this branch of medicine had fallen in the rear of its kindred branches, and that a knowledge of it was of the highest importance to the medical practitioner, his energies were devoted to the effort to restore it to its right position, and there is no doubt that his exertions contributed largely to revolutionize the system of instruction then existing in the University, and soon to bring about a change which in other hands placed the department of pharmacology in the front rank of medical instruction.

But there was another field with which Dr. Jackson was occupied, in cultivating which, all the traits of his constitutional nature and his talents were fully exhibited. In 1822, he had been elected one of the "attending physicians of the Philadelphia Almshouse." This establishment then, as it now does, presented the most extensive opportunities for the observation of disease, and for pathological research. Since its resources had by enlightened direction a few years previously been made available for clinical purposes, it constituted an invaluable school of study and improvement, not only for students of medicine, but for the rising generation of medical men. By Dr. Jackson, such opportunities were seized with ardor; he had become an indefatigable student and reader, and he neglected no occasion of verifying his knowledge derived from books, or of correcting preconceived ideas if not borne out by facts presented in his bedside investigation. At the time specified, practical medicine was in a state of probation, an active inquiring spirit had pervaded every portion of it, and the old theories and modes of exploration challenged re-examination. If we search into the causes of this activity, they must be recognized in the diffusion of intelligence through the periodical medical press that had been established, which,

not waiting for the developments of learned societies, or the
slow experiences of authors through erudite treatises, scattered
broadcast the accounts of disease in particular localities, the
results of even the humblest investigators in science, gathered
up communications from foreign sources, and enabled each one
to inform himself in the speediest way concerning all that was
pertinent to the immediate subject of his thoughts and requirements. In this species of enterprise our own country had set
the example.[1]

Without attempting to enumerate all the advances in practical medicine that had been brought about, or were being
inaugurated, we may allude to a few in which Dr. Jackson was
especially interested, and which he contributed to render
effective. The mode of arriving at an accurate diagnosis of
diseases of the chest by means of auscultation had within a few
years been devised by Laennec. This distinguished patho-
logist and practitioner, instigated by some passages in the works
of Hippocrates with reference to employing the ear in the de-
tection of sounds connected with disease of the lungs, and
deriving his cue further from the work of Avenbrugger upon
the availability of assisting diagnosis by percussion, invented
the method of studying pectoral affections by means of "mediate auscultation."[2] To him we are indebted for devising the
stethoscope, and for all the brilliant results of the discovery
that a sure and certain method existed by which discrimina-
tion between such diseases was as practicable as if they were
submitted to inspection.

In the light of the present day, when this mode of exploration has been carried to such refinement of application, it
would appear extraordinary that it had been overlooked for so
long a period, and at this the discoverer himself expressed his
astonishment. In 1818, he read a memoir upon the subject to
the Academy of Sciences of Paris, and in the same year published his work entitled, "On Mediate Auscultation; or, A

---

[1] The "Medical Repository," of New York, was published in 1797. It
took precedence of the Medical Journals of Europe. See Rev. Dr. Miller's Life of Edward Miller, M.D.

[2] He had been a pupil of Corvisart, who was in the habit of listening to
the sounds of the heart.

Treatise on the Diagnosis of the Lungs and of the Heart, based principally upon this new mode of Exploration." It is not necessary to narrate how this revelation was received in Europe; the story has been told by the English translator of the work, the eminent Dr. John Forbes; it will be more to the purpose to exhibit the reception it met with in the United States.

When Dr. Jackson became a visiting physician of the Almshouse, auscultation was in its infancy, and it became his duty, as well as a pleasure, from the extreme interest he took in it, to test its value and develop its practical usefulness. With the younger men who were associated with him in charge of the sick wards, he studied diligently the cases under treatment, applied the method of diagnosis that he had introduced among them, and where death occurred verified the results of their previous estimates of disease by pathological examination. He was a student as well as teacher among students. The first fruits of this laborious employment were given in the form of an Inaugural Essay, printed in the May number of the Philadelphia Journal of Medical and Physical Sciences for 1824, by Dr. Edmund Strudwick, of North Carolina, one of the resident students of the Almshouse. In this essay he refers to Dr. Jackson's guidance.

We are told, in the life of Laennec by Dr. Forbes, that in England this discovery " was at first received by the profession with considerable distrust, and the new mode of diagnosis, and especially the instrument, was attempted to be turned into ridicule." It has been stated that the discovery of the circulation of the blood was not received by any physician of the time of Harvey who was over forty years of age, and this may be said to have been the case as regards the introduction of mediate auscultation in this country. It was opposed by even those who from their studies of the vocal apparatus ought to have taken a more favorable view of it. It was subjected to derision, and a paraphrase of Dr. Johnson's definition of the angler was freely circulated : "A patient at one end of a wooden tube and a fool at the other." I recollect the case of a gentleman laboring under phthisis, whose wife was desirous that an examination of him should be made with the stethoscope, and on making the request of the physician in attendance, he replied he would get her one and she could make the examination herself. But this incredulity and ignorance were destined to disappear before the advancing march of science. Adepts arose whose skill and precision swept from before them all doubt and sarcasm. A pertinent illustration of what was then regarded as a triumphant vindication of the precision of stethoscopic diagnosis was related to me by the late Dr. Samuel George Morton, to which he was a witness: a person at the head of the police force of this city, a man of great muscular development and robust constitution, had so injured his health by dissipation and exposure as to present all the rational signs of consumption least expected in such a subject; the attending physicians were no believers in physical exploration, and Dr. Jackson was called in to test his skill, and see if he could elucidate the real condition of the patient. He diagnosticated an extensive vomica and gave its "metes and bounds." Post-mortem examination verified to a tittle the accuracy of the diagnosis, and auscultation had a new significance in the eyes of the spectators.

Upon the reorganization of the Board of Physicians and Surgeons of the Almshouse in 1822, including three professors of the University, the system was introduced of delivering lectures regularly on Wednesdays and Saturdays in the lecture-room. These lectures soon became extremely popular, and attracted large classes of medical students annually; their popularity in no small degree arose from the devoted earnestness and lucid expositions of Dr. Jackson. His effectiveness and force as a clinical teacher were maintained throughout the prolonged period that he was connected with this infirmary, from which he retired in 1845, when coerced by more pressing duties. His clinical teaching was afterwards confined wholly to that service within the walls of the University. Several of his clinical lectures delivered in the Philadelphia (Almshouse) Hospital are published in the early numbers of the Medical Examiner.

In 1827 Dr. Jackson was chosen by Professor Chapman as his assistant in the University. The Chair embraced the "Theory and Practice of Medicine, Clinical Medicine, and the Institutes of Medicine." The delivery of lectures upon the latter of these subjects was delegated to the assistant.

The branch of "Institutes of Medicine" has met with varied
fortunes as regards its position of subserviency or independence in this school of medicine. It was originally appended to the chair of chemistry, having been recommended
by Dr. Wistar, then a member of the Board of Trustees,
but elected in 1789 the incumbent of a twofold chair of
chemistry and institutes. In the arrangement that was rendered necessary by the coalition of the College and the University in 1791, it was desirable to accommodate both Dr. Kuhn
and Dr. Rush, and the theory and practice was therefore appor-
tioned to the former professor, while the subject of the institutes conjoined to clinical medicine was assumed by the latter.
When Dr. Kuhn resigned, Dr. Rush succeeded to the chair of
the theory and practice, into which were merged clinical medicine and the institutes. It thus stood at the time of Dr. Jackson's appointment.

However brilliant had been the discourses of the eloquent
Rush, the times had changed as regards the requirements of
medical teaching, and the development of physiological and
pathological science demanded additional assistance in doing
justice to subjects included under so comprehensive a title as
that held by Professor Chapman. It has been seen how clinical medicine had been provided for in a school of experience
where the professor of practice had so able an assistant in Dr.
Jackson, and now he was selected by the same professor to aid
him in his collegiate duties. Practical medicine had been carried to an exalted position in the courses of instruction, but Dr.
Chapman had found himself unable to meet the requirements
of a more extended sphere and the institutes were discontinued.

In the discourse that was delivered by Dr. Jackson, when
entering upon the duties of his appointment, he indicated the
topics falling properly within the circle of the institutes, and
laid down the principles upon which rational medicine is based.
Physiology, pathology, therapeutics, symptomatology, semeio-
sis, diagnosis, prognosis, and hygiene are designated as the subjects comprised in this general term of institutes, in the discussion of which adherence to a rigid system of philosophic reasoning is strictly to be maintained. He pointed out the difference

2

between theory and hypothesis, and indicated the true value of experience. His axiom must be admitted to be correct: "Experience combined with sound discriminating observation furnishes the facts from which theory is derived, while the truth of theory can be alone determined by experience and observation." This embraces the true elements of the Baconian system. In endeavoring to carry out his ideal conceptions of the task he had undertaken, he drew his materials from all the available resources at his command, and spared no pains or labor to render his efforts effectual. I was one of those who attended his first course of lectures, and can fully testify not only to its entire acceptableness to those who listened to him, but to the pleasure that was derived from his earnestness of address and his eloquent style of delivery. Restricted as he was for time, as only two lectures a week were allotted to him, and that in a session of but four months' duration, this course was but the foreshadowing of what his lectures became in subsequent years, when occupying the position of full professor.

At the time that Dr. Jackson had fully entered upon his career as a medical teacher, there arose a brilliant light in the firmament of medical science in the person of Broussais. This distinguished innovator has been overshadowed and has almost been forgotten in the advances that have been made in the last thirty years; but we must refer to him as one who was all potent in swaying the opinions and in influencing the practice of those who were the recipients of his instruction, or who, through his numerous publications, became convinced of the correctness of his innovations. At the present day the idea of Broussaisism is connected with gastro-enteritis as the source of all febrile diseases, and with leeches and gum-water as remedies to be employed in combating them. No such impression can be more erroneous. Broussais was a philosopher as well as an innovator, and, as the founder of what has been termed the "Physiological System of Medicine," he is entitled to the highest respect and admiration. His "Researches upon Hectic Fever," but more especially his "History of Chronic Inflammations," which had reached its fourth edition in 1826, had placed him in the front rank of

medical observers.[1] But his "Treatise on Physiology applied
to Pathology,"[2] and his "Examination of the Medical Doctrine
generally adopted, and the Modern Systems of Nosology," had
placed him still higher as a systematic inquirer into the
general principles on which our science is founded. His
efforts were directed to break down the Ontology that existed,
and to establish in its place a system of demonstration and
reasoning founded on the structure and vital operations of the
organs, their modes of impressibility, and their relations to one
another. With him originated the expression that life was
"organism in action;" and he asserted that this action was
maintained through the excitability pertaining to the tissues
and organs — that morbid excitability was *irritability*, and
morbid excitation was *irritation*.

It is not possible for us to trace out in detail the full bearing
of the doctrines of Broussais, or the influence they have had
upon the medical mind; but we must admit the correctness
of the estimate that has been given by one of his biogra-
phers with respect to his services to medical science, when
he states, that, while his effort to establish a system was a pure
conception of his mind, his glory originated from another
source, the practical impulse that he gave to the researches of
the new medical generation, by reason of which he has led
us all to the study of organic lesions, to the search for local
diagnosis, and the true interpretation of symptoms.[3] Dr. Jackson was deeply imbued with the importance of Broussais's
teachings, and he gave in his adhesion to the "School of
Physiological Medicine." He not only taught medicine in
accordance with the inculcations of this philosophy, but advocated in debate the truthfulness of the developments that had
been made by it.[4]

[1] This book was translated from the French by Isaac Hays, M.D., and
R. Egglesfield Griffith, M.D., 1831.
[2] This work was translated from the French by John Bell, M.D., and
R. La Roche, M.D., Philadelphia, 1826.
[3] Eloges lus dans les Séances Publiques de l'Academie, par E. Fred.
Dubois (d'Amiens). Paris, 1864.
[4] In the "Philadelphia Journal of the Medical and Physical Sciences"
for 1826 and 1827, will be found a series of essays by Dr. Jackson, in which
he gives, first, an admirable account of the progress of the doctrine of irri-

The winter of 1830-31 was remarkable for the interest that was awakened by the public discussion of medical topics in the " Medical Society of Philadelphia." This Society was composed of senior and junior members,—the latter consisting of students of the two medical schools. The champions of opposing views were Dr. Jackson, and Dr. Daniel Drake, late of Cincinnati, who for a season held the chair of Institutes and Practice of Medicine in the Jefferson Medical College.[1] From week to week expectation was on tiptoe as each one read his paper, and in the debate which followed met the objections and criticisms of his antagonist. It was the school of the philosophers renewed. Dr. Jackson there exhibited his profound knowledge of his subject, his erudition and broad views of medical science, supported by his own clinical experience and deductions, and he came out of the encounter with enhanced reputation, although it was sustained with one of the most accomplished and practiced debaters that have ever arisen in the medical profession. It was no mean distinction to have triumphantly maintained his positions when Professor Drake was in opposition. While all who were listeners were deeply interested, the enthusiasm of the juvenile portion of the audience was at its acme.

It is not to be understood, however, that Dr. Jackson was a blind partisan of the school of Broussais; his appreciation of him was modified by a correct knowledge of the scope of medicine. In speaking of this leader, he remarks: " The doctrine of Broussais, evolved by his extensive pathological researches and clinical observations, combined with a method often of rigid induction, allies the principle of Brown with the general anatomy of Bichat. This doctrine in its fullest extent can be considered, however, as no more than the physiology and philosophy of irritation. This great and extended pheno-

tability from the earliest times. He then presents the different characteristics assumed by irritation in the several tissues and organs of the economy, and traces the laws by which it is governed. At the time these papers were published they were invaluable, not only as an exposition of the stage at which medical knowledge had arrived, but from the suggestive thought contained in them.

[1] Dr. Jackson was one of the Vice-Presidents of the Medical Society.

menon, productive of so many and diversified consequences, he has appreciated more clearly and developed more fully than any who have preceded him. This system is, however, not perfect; it is not universal. Physiological knowledge lies far in the rear of that state of perfection to which it will arrive; the mysteries of vital phenomena, the laws of vital activity, no one can pretend are spread before us in a blaze of light, leaving no doubt, no hesitancies, no difficulties as to their nature. For no system of physiological medicine can there be claimed the attributes of infallibility and perfection. The system of Broussais contains many and important truths, but it is not all true, nor does it compass all truth. It is enforced by its author in too dogmatical a spirit."[1]

At this time pathological investigation had another notable promoter in the person of Louis. This remarkable man was the opposite of Broussais in characteristics, for he was quiet and unassuming; long reticent as regards the results of the inquiries that occupied him, when they had been attained he gave them to the world to be judged by the only true test of discovery, their confirmation or disproval by others. Louis was no litigant; by long toil and patience he had rent the veil which concealed the correct pathology of typhoid fever, and with his former master, Chomel, gave such a comprehensive detailed account of the disease as to carry conviction to the minds of all impartial pathologists that the imputation of obscurity existed no longer. It could not be denied that the structural lesions of the "slow nervous fever" of Huxham, of the "mucous fever" of Stoll, and of the "lingering remittents" whose persistency and phenomena had for so long a time embarrassed the practitioner, and baffled his attempts at speedy cure, had been at last determined.[2]

---

[1] Preface to the Principles of Medicine, p. ix.

[2] The book of Louis is entitled—

"Recherches Anatomiques, Pathologiques et Therapeutiques sur le Maladies connues sous les noms de Gastro-Enterite, Fievre Putride, Adynamique, Ataxique, Typhoide, etc., par P. Ch. A. Louis, M.D., etc. etc., 1829." Louis informs us in his preface that he was engaged in gathering together his materials for this work from 1822 to 1827. It was published two years afterwards.

It is interesting to review the time when what is now among the settled truths of pathological science was passing through the period of rigid scrutiny; when awakened inquirers were struggling for enlightenment. Of this great discovery Dr. Jackson was not unmindful, but he had not disabused himself of the purely gastro-enteritic origin of fevers; he had not taken in the true fact, that the glands of Peyer and Bruner were the seats of the organic lesions in this form of febrile disease. I recollect at the commencement of my novitiate, as resident physician of the Philadelphia Almshouse in 1830, that Dr. Jackson, standing by the bedside of a patient, whose disease was a persistent fever, and descanting upon its probable pathology before a class of students, referred to the views and the investigations of Louis, and remarked that in this disease that observer had determined an inflammation more particularly restricted to the caput coli. With these hints, and with the works of Louis and Chomel that soon came into our hands, we were not slow by practical investigation in realizing the truth of their statements.[1] Through the guidance of these authorities,

---

[1] The occurrence of ulcerations in the intestines in connection with fever had been noticed by a number of observers. In 1814 Petit & Serres published an account of a form of fever, called "fievre entero-mesentérique ;" they noticed the ulcerations. Trolier of the Hôtel Dieu, of Lyons, refers to ulcers in the intestines in cases of fever (Archives Générales, Sept. 1825, Vol. IX.). Bretonneau, having observed the same lesion in the intestines, gave to it the name of "Dothinenterite." (Archiv. Gen., and N. A. Med. and Surg. Journ., July, 1826.) Dr. George B. Wood refers to a case of perforation of the ileum, and ulceration in typhus mitior. (Art. on Oil of turpentine, etc., N. A. Med. and Surg. Journ., April 1826.) Dr. Hewitt, of London, noticed ulceration of the intestines without attributing more importance to the fact than as complicating fever. (Lond. Med. Phys. Journal, Aug. 1827.) Dr. Geo. Bettner reported " Cases of ulcerations of the intestines in connection with fever," observed by him when a resident of the Philadelphia Almshouse. (N. A. Med. and Surg. Journ. 1828.) In his "Clinical Illustrations of fever, 1830," Dr. Alexander Tweedie notices the ulceration in "typhus fever" and specifies 16 cases out of 54 dissections ; he also alludes to the enlargement of the mesenteric glands. In the systematic treatises on the practice of medicine, no reference was made to the pathology of typhoid fever. Gregory who published in 1828-29, Southwood Smith in 1830, and Eberle whose work was issued in 1831, made no allusion to the ulceration of the intestines. Until the appearance of the work of Louis in 1829, and that of Chomel in 1834, there was no recognition of the fact that in typhoid fever there existed an essential form typical as regards symptoms, course, and anatomical

the lesions of "typhoid fever" became perfectly familiar to us, and I need only further state that with this foundation perfected by a service with Louis himself in Paris, my late lamented colleague, Dr. Gerhard, most conclusively drew the distinction between bilious, remittent, typhus, and typhoid fevers. His conclusions have become the settled facts of medical science.[1]

In 1832 was published the "Principles of Medicine founded on the structure and functions of the animal organism." This work has been subjected to varied criticism, occasionally severe, according, for the most part, to the preconceived views and fixed opinions of the reviewer. It is necessary, therefore, to give an account of the circumstances under which it was issued. At the time Dr. Jackson undertook the task of teaching the institutes of medicine, the subject was in a disarranged condition. A new foundation for the prosecution of physiological and pathological inquiry had been laid by the labors of Bichat at the commencement of the century, and the spirit of research that was engendered, while it bore ample fruits, as we have seen in the contributions of Laennec and Broussais, was equally prolific of revelations through the genius and untiring devotion of Andral, of Chomel, and of Louis. The "Anatomie Générale" of Bichat was extended by the zeal and faithfulness of Meckel and Béclard, while special experimenters endeavored to comprehend the uses of

intestinal lesions, which had been partially depicted by Huxham as the "slow nervous fever," the typhus mitior of other writers. An account of typhoid fever was published in the American edition of Mackintosh's Practice in 1835, written by Dr. Carson. It is due to the memory of the late Dr. James Jackson, Jr., of Boston, to state that, when in 1833 he returned from Paris, he recognized, in an epidemic of what was supposed to be typhus, the same lesions he had seen when a pupil of Louis. (Memoir by his father, Dr. James Jackson.) Ulceration of the intestines was observed in New England by Dr. Bartlett and other physicians. (Bartlett on Typhoid and Typhus Fever, 1842.)

[1] Upon his return from Europe, Dr. Gerhard undertook the task of determining the identity of the typhoid fever of this country and that of France, and also of ascertaining the true pathological distinction between it and the bilious, remittent, and typhus fevers. This he did in the Pennsylvania Hospital, and in the Philadelphia Hospital (Almshouse). His papers are contained in the American Journal of the Medical Sciences, Feb. 1835; Feb. 1837; August, 1837.

the several tissues and organs, their relations and dependence upon one another, and their laws of operation. Magendie, Sir Charles Bell, and others had made new discoveries, which had shed a flood of light upon the obscure processes of life, and materially changed the conceptions entertained with respect to the phenomena of disease. Nor was this all; the physicists and chemists, directing their attention to the natural forces, and to the chemical changes of the material elements of the body, had opened a field of exploration and research which gave a new aspect to practical medicine. Of what avail were these to the student of medicine? They were as a dead letter for want of the medium of acquirement and comprehension. We had no comprehensive text-books then, as now, in every department of medical science. We were dependent upon our lecturers alone for leading us into the right paths of study and reflection. The attempt of Dr. Jackson was to co-ordinate all the materials at his command that bore upon the subject for the instruction of his pupils, to lay a foundation for their subsequent progress in the acquisition of knowledge, and when, after a few years of experience in teaching, he printed his lectures, he did a good work in the cause of educational advancement. Students felt this, although mature practitioners were annoyed and perplexed at the "jargon of the schools" which has since become a living nomenclature.

The work of Dr. Jackson performed its mission: it was an elementary book of general scope, and when scores of laborious systematic compilers had spread their productions broadcast, and the student was no longer at a loss for condensed sources of knowledge, the necessity of revising and continuing it no longer existed. From the advance of science, to have revised this work would have been to rewrite it, and he permitted it to be superseded.

There is one point on which I would desire to fix attention. The fact of reflex action existing as a power in the structure of the nervous system, and the demonstration of its manifestations, being due to Marshall Hall, of England, to Müller, of Germany, and to our own countryman Campbell, are well known to the profession; yet it is satisfactory to present an evidence of how far an elementary work of 1832 recognized this physiological principle. After giving the phenomena upon which the evidence is based, Dr. Jackson remarks: "In these examples is manifested an excitement transmitted by nervous communication from one organ in which it is developed to another organ to which it is transported—to which it is imparted. It may then be regarded as a positive fact that the nervous tissue possesses, as a functional capacity, the power of transmission, a species of radiation, by the action of which an impression, a stimulation, a mode of activity imparted to a tissue or an organ is communicated to distant organs."

"An irritation or stimulation, the excitation of the organic actions, awakens the activity of the transmitting faculty of the nervous tissue and is conveyed and repeated in the nervous centres, disturbing their mode of existence, and consequently through them is *reflected* into other organs or tissues with which these centres are in communication. This fact is displayed in convulsions, which may be induced in highly sensitive individuals by excessive tickling." Here, then, is the expression, though in general terms, of an association between the organs through the medium of the reflex capabilities, which, in explanation of the energies and sympathies, has been experimentally illustrated and defined with precision by the researches of Hall, Müller and Bernard, of Schiff and Brown-Séquard, and their co-laborers.[1]

The year 1832 was another remarkable one in the medical annals of Philadelphia, and indeed it may be stated of this continent and of Europe. For several years previously Asiatic cholera had been pursuing a steady and fatal course from east to west over the fair and populous countries of the globe. Early in 1831 it had prevailed in Eastern Europe,

---

[1] With respect to the phenomenon of reflex action noticed by Marshall Hall in the tail of an eel, when separated from the body, that writer says: " I soon found similar observations had been recorded by various physiological writers, Redi, Whytt, Prochaska, Mr. Mayo, etc. But I observed that in their hands they had remained useless and sterile, having led to no conclusions, having neither been traced backwards to any physiological principle of action, nor forward to any function of the animal economy. I conceived it impossible that any such phenomenon should exist in nature without such connections, and I resolved to pursue the subject.'' First Memoir read before the Royal Society, 1833. Second Memoir in 1837.

and, slowly progressing, by the commencement of the following year it had included France and England in its stretch, and awakened with the people of America anxious forebodings of its invasion. Here, the public mind was fully aroused to the threatened danger, and in April a communication was addressed by the Board of Health to the Philadelphia Medical Society, recommending the appointment of a committee "to institute an examination into all the facts in relation to the epidemic cholera, and to report in detail the result of their investigation, for the benefit and satisfaction of the unprofessional as well as the medical part of the community." In accordance with this request a committee was appointed, consisting of Drs. Condie, Emerson, Hays, Jackson, Bond, Horner, and Huston. The report which was submitted by these gentlemen was deemed so valuable that it was ordered to be printed and extensively circulated. But the action of the authorities did not stop here. In anticipation of a visitation of the disease, which had now reached the American continent, a Sanitary Board of Councils had been appointed, which, on June 22d, 1832, passed the following resolution: "Resolved, that it is expedient that three physicians of eminence be appointed to proceed forthwith to Montreal or Quebec or both, at their discretion, to ascertain the true nature of the disease prevailing there, and to obtain such further information in relation thereto as they may deem necessary, and to make their communication as early as practicable to the Board."

"The Board appointed Samuel Jackson, Charles D. Meigs, and Richard Harlan."

The commission proceeded immediately to the performance of their delegated duty. They visited Montreal and thoroughly investigated all the circumstances connected with the outbreak of the disease in that locality. They designated the disease as "malignant cholera," and observed its phases and their peculiar phenomena. The information collected by them was embodied in a report which bears the date of July 8th, 1832. It was none too early for its beneficial influence, for the pest had already reached New York, and in the closing period of the month began to desolate this city.

In the fierce encounter with this new invader of the peace

and prosperity of their fellow-citizens the members of the medical profession evinced their courage and endurance; the part enacted by them constitutes the story that has been told by the historians of the period. The school-houses and places that could be found suitable in convenient portions of the city were converted into hospitals, under the charge of the leading prominent physicians, while their younger colleagues shared in the care, the fatigue, and watching entailed upon them. Each of the members of the commission referred to had a position in chief in connection with these establishments, and, as the services rendered were gratuitous, received, with others, as a token of gratitude and of commemoration from the city, a silver pitcher, on which was engraved a fit record of the purpose of the donation and of the occasion of its bestowal.

Dr. Jackson had charge of City Cholera Hospital No. 5. He published two elaborate papers on the subject of Malignant Cholera, in the February and May numbers of the " American Journal of the Medical Sciences" for 1833. They are of a practical character as regards the nature of the disease, and its pathology and treatment, and illustrated by the report of thirty-three cases.

In 1835 changes were made in the organization of the University. The chair of Materia Medica having been vacated, and a new Professor elected in the person of Dr. Wood, it was deemed expedient as well as just that the chair of Institutes should be re-established, and that branch again be placed on an independent footing. This was due to Dr. Jackson, who had made his record while assistant lecturer; and now the way was clear before him for the enlarged display of his eminent abilities, and for the increase of his popularity and usefulness.

Science and knowledge cannot be stationary; no matter how stagnant the sources may become at certain periods, choked as it were by supine apathy, or the influence of dogmatic authority, there are latent natural powers always in existence which must sooner or later be put in operation to restore the purity and freshness of the current. This has been the case in medicine. At the termination of the last century, experimental investigation was at a stand; the authority of Cullen had superseded that of Boerhaave, and vital solidism had universally been accepted in place of the mechanical philosophy. But a new era was at hand, for John Hunter had not exhausted or even gone to the depths of experimental truth; by Bichat and Nysten life was exhibited from new stand-points; and then came forth those brilliant revelations that have placed the name of Magendie among the leaders in physiological science. The humoral system had assumed a new and more rational aspect under the moulding hand of expert chemists.

When Dr. Jackson entered upon the functions of his chair, physiological science had so far advanced as to render the explanation of the connection between the organs by unmeaning sympathy no longer tolerated. The direct agents of communication between them had been made so clear and demonstrable as to command conviction, while the direct influence of agents upon the animal economy, by their absorption, so long denied, was proved beyond the possibility of cavil; and further, microscopic research was shedding anew its wonderful disclosures, not only as regards healthy structural formation of the tissues, but as to their pathological metamorphoses.[1] The business of the Professor of the Institutes was to gather up, from all available resources, everything that elucidated the nature of life-actions of the organism; to search into the laws that governed them, and then to place a distinct account of the facts and principles he had gleaned before his pupils. As year upon year rolled by, this duty he continued faithfully and eloquently to fulfil, and never fell behind the knowledge which the fertile spirit of inquiry was constantly imparting.

A feature that was prominent in Dr. Jackson's mental constitution was openness to conviction; he was not permanently wedded to any preconceived opinion or hypothesis, for he was willing to modify and even change his views in accordance with discovery. In the early enunciation of his ideas upon medicine, it is evident his bias was towards the vitalistic doc-

[1] In a communication entitled "Thoughts on Sympathy, in a Letter from Charles Caldwell, M.D., to N. Chapman, M.D.," in the third volume of Philadelphia Journal of the Medical and Physical Sciences, the experiments and their results upon absorption then in progress were stigmatized as "efforts to reinundate the world with the foul tide of humoral doctrines."

trine; but, as facts accumulated and thought expanded under the declarations of the physicists and chemists, he found that exclusiveness did not comport with truth, and he fully recognized the value of their labors. Let me elucidate by reference to the "correlation of forces."

The hypothesis that life actions are intimately associated with and dependent upon physical forces, although traceable through bygone times of medical history, has received new importance from the experiments of physical explorers with respect to the connection between the forces of nature themselves. These forces are everywhere in operation, and constitute the moving powers of inorganic as well as of organic matter. The identity of these forces, or, in other words, their mutual conversion, has been propounded, and evidence adduced to sustain the supposition of the production of one through the instrumentality of another. In this line of inquiry and speculation, Biot, Arago, Herschel, Faraday, Matteucci, and Grove have been distinguished. The extension of the same mode of resolving movements has been ingeniously applied to the organic world. In 1845 Mayer, of Hilbron, published his paper, in Germany, upon the correlation and identity of physical and vital forces; and in 1850 the subject was ably discussed by Dr. Carpenter, in a communication to the Royal Society of London. It is worthy of note, that as early as 1821 a paper on this subject was published in this country by the late Dr. Godman, entitled "Some observations on the propriety of explaining the actions of the animal economy by the assistance of the physical sciences;" to the correlation of forces, however, no allusion is made.

In an introductory lecture published in 1837, Dr. Jackson thus expresses himself: "All the phenomena of organization, physiological or pathological, are thus referable, like all other phenomena of nature, to a small category of general laws. Physical phenomena, according to the class they belong to, are referred to a few simple laws, as of gravity, caloric, of affinity, of galvanism, of electricity, of magnetism, *all of which it can now be scarcely doubted, are themselves but modifications of one great law of force.* The force producing physiological or organic phenomena may be no more than a modification of the same ruling power displaying its activity in organized matter; strong analogics could be advanced to sustain this view."

In a subsequent lecture (1851) this subject is discussed by him *in extenso*. In this he draws the distinction between pure life force and the physical forces, and maintains that the special character of organic or "radical force of life" is modality, or the power of creating organic forms, the instruments and mechanism of life. "It possesses none of the attributes of the physical forces in its actions and influences. It has no identity with them, yet there is undoubted correlation." "Germ force and organic force are identical." He dissents from the views expressed by Dr. Carpenter in his admirably suggestive discussion of life forces, that "just as heat, light, chemical affinity, etc., are transformable into vital force, so is vital force capable of manifesting itself in the production of light, heat, chemical affinity or mechanical motion." Dr. Jackson maintained the separate and independent existence of a vital force, operating on and obeying the influences of the physical, but not identical with or convertible into them; with him the dependence of life force upon physical forces, to maintain its existence, and to secure the metamorphic changes connected with typical permanency and evolution of organic structure, constitutes the correlation.

In addition to membership in the societies that have been referred to, Dr. Jackson was also a member of the College of Physicians, and of the American Philosophical Society. In 1836 the "Académie Royale de Médecine" of France conferred on him the honor of corresponding membership.

In 1863 Dr. Jackson resigned his professorship, after having performed its duties for twenty-eight years, and having been connected with the University during the long period of thirty-six years. During the latter half of his life his constitution was not robust, nor were his physical powers vigorous. He had for many years been the subject of neuralgia, which subjected him to great suffering, and ultimately loss of locomotor capability was so decided as to become ataxic. But he toiled on to the last moment of bodily endurance; and when only old age coerced retirement from active scenes he withdrew entirely from them. In the latter epoch of his life the maxim of Cicero appears to have been adopted by him. "Pugnandum tanquam contra morbum, sic contra senectutem." His last medical communication was written in 1870. He died April 4th, 1872, at the age of eighty-five years.

I have thus endeavored to sketch the career of one who, while engaged in the great drama of this world's concerns, played a conspicuous part. His memory should be cherished not solely for his effective co-operation in the work of medical education, and his hearty sympathy with the scientific impulse of the time, but for his good deeds, and for his whole-souled devotion to the claims inseparable from humanity. With the graduates of the University of Pennsylvania, who knew his worth and loved his virtues, there must remain the tenderest recollections of their preceptor and their friend.

PAPERS PUBLISHED BY DR. JACKSON.

An Account of the Yellow or Malignant Fever which appeared in the city of Philadelphia in the summer and autumn of 1820, with some Observations on that Disease. By Samuel Jackson, M.D., President of the Board of Health. Philadelphia Journal of the Medical and Physical Sciences, vol. i. No. 2, vol. ii. Nos. 1 and 2, 1820–21, three papers.

On the Condition of the Medicines of the United States, and the means of their reform. An Introductory Lecture delivered in the Philadelphia College of Pharmacy. Phil. Journ. of Med. and Phys. Sciences, vol. v. No. 2. 1822.

Case of Pulmonary Disease attended with some anomalous Symptoms, ibid., vol. 7. 1823.

Case of Effusion into the Chest, in which Paracentesis was performed, ibid., New Series, vol. 1, 1825.

On Vitality and Vital Forces, ibid., vol. 13, 1826.

The Doctrine of Irritation, ibid., vol. 13, 1826.

Laws of Irritation, a continuation of the preceding, ibid., vol. 10, iv. 1827.

On James's Fever Powder. Journal of the Philadelphia College of Pharmacy, May, 1826.

Cases of Nervous Irritation exhibiting the efficacy of cold as a remedy. North American Med. and Surg. Journal, vol. 2. October, 1826.

Statement of the Effects of Swaim's Panacea, appended to a Report of the Philadelphia Medical Society. North American Med. and Surg. Journ., vol. 5, Jan. 1828.

Clinical Reports of Cases treated in the Infirmary of the Almshouse of the city and county of Philadelphia. American Journal of Med. Sci., vol. i., Nov. 1827.

Case of Gastro-Meningeal Irritation, caused by Metastasis, ibid., May, 1828.

Case of Amnesia, ibid., Feb. 1829.

Clinical Reports of Cases treated in the Infirmary of the Almshouse of the city and county of Philadelphia, ibid., Feb. 1829.

Case of Tetanus. Respiration performed by one lung, etc., ibid., Feb. 1829.

Cases of Cynanche Trachealis, ibid., Aug. 1829.

On Absorption, ibid., Feb. 1830.

On the Pulse and its Modifications, ibid., May, 1830.

Observations on Hematosis, with two cases in which this function was imperfectly performed, ibid., May, 1830.

On the Pathology or Abnormal State of the Circulation, ibid., Aug. 1830.

Personal Observations and Experience of Epidemic or Malignant Cholera in the city of Philadelphia in 1832, ibid., Feb. and May, 1833, two papers.

Case of Intussusception, ibid., Aug. 1833.

On Medical Education, ibid., Feb. 1834. An Introductory Lecture.

Preface to Cases of Yellow Fever. By E. B. Harris, M.D., of New Orleans, ibid., May, 1834.

Case of Purpura Hæmorrhagica, ibid., May, 1834.

Obscure Pericarditis, Dilatation of the Heart, Peculiar Species of Tumor on the Right and Left Ventricles and Left Auricle, Œdema of the Fauces, Larynx, and Glottis, Death from Suffocation, ibid., Feb. 1835.

Observations on Hydrophobia, with Cases, in one of which Chloroform was administered with a favorable result, ibid., April, 1849.

Case in which a large quantity of Chloroform was used, ibid., April, 1849.

On the Influence upon Health of the Introduction of Tea and Coffee in large proportion into the Dietary of Children and the Laboring Classes, ibid., July, 1849.

Digestion of Fatty Matters by the Pancreatic Juice, ibid., Oct. 1854.

A Discourse commemorative of Nathaniel Chapman, M.D., late Professor of the Theory and Practice of Medicine and of Clinical Medicine; delivered before the Trustees, Medical Faculty, and Students of the University of Pennsylvania, October 13, 1854.

On the Functions of the different Parts of the Internal Ear, Am. Journ. Med. Sciences, April, 1856.

On Starch as a Product of the Liver, and on the Amyloid Degeneration of the Liver in Yellow Fever, ibid., vol. 34, new series, Oct. 1857.

On Therapeutic Applications of the Solution of Permanganate of Potash and Ozone, ibid., vol. 49, Jan. 1864, N. S.

On the Uses of Sugar and Lactic Acid on the economy, ibid., vol. 49, April, 1865.

Cases of Inflammation occurring under Peculiar Conditions, with some Thoughts and Reflections on the Nature, Constitution, and Purposes of this organic process in the Animal Organism, ibid., vol. 55, Jan. 1868.

Case of Derangement limited to a single moral sentiment, occurring periodically, that sentiment being in a perfectly normal condition during the intervals, ibid., vol. 55, April, 1868.

On Consciousness and Cases of so-called Double Consciousness, ibid., vol. 56, Jan. 1869.

A Rare Disease of the Joints, ibid., vol. 60, July, 1870.